The
MAYFLOWER

Author Libby Romero
Illustrator Olga Baumert .
Senior Editor Shannon Beatty
Editor Sophie Parkes
Senior Art Editor Claire Patane
Designer Eleanor Bates
Editorial Assistant Becky Walsh
Subject Consultant Tom Begley, Plimoth Plantation
Senior Production Editor Nikoleta Parasaki
Senior Production Controller Inderjit Bhullar
Jacket Coordinator Isobel Walsh
Picture Researcher Sakshi Saluja
Managing Editor Penny Smith
Managing Art Editor Mabel Chan
Creative Director Helen Senior
Publishing Director Sarah Larter

First published in Great Britain in 2020 by
Dorling Kindersley Limited
80 Strand, London, WC2R 0RL

Copyright © 2020 Dorling Kindersley Limited
A Penguin Random House Company
10 9 8 7 6 5 4 3 2 1
001–316419–Jul/2020

A CIP catalogue record for this book
is available from the British Library.
ISBN: 978-0-2414-0959-6

Printed in China

A WORLD OF IDEAS:
SEE ALL THERE IS TO KNOW

www.dk.com

FSC
www.fsc.org
MIX
Paper from
responsible sources
FSC™ C018179

Introduction

Welcome to the story of the *Mayflower*!

Within these pages you will read about the exciting voyage of the *Mayflower*. Discover the remarkable events that took place when the Pilgrims travelled across the ocean to America.

Find out why the Pilgrims left Europe in the first place, and what happened when they reached Plymouth, their new home. Learn about who they met there, and how the events that happened over the first harsh winter changed the course of American history.

Discover the real story of the first Thanksgiving, and how it shaped the America we know today.

PLIMOTH® PLANTATION

Contents

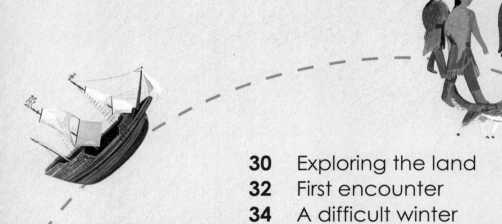

England

Where it all began

In March 1590, William Bradford was born into a family of farmers in Austerfield, England. When he was a young boy, both of his parents and his grandparents died, so he went to live with his uncles.

Bradford was a sickly child, so he couldn't work in the fields. Instead, he spent his days reading the Bible. He thought a lot about how people around him worshipped God. By the time he was 12, he knew he wanted something different.

William Bradford

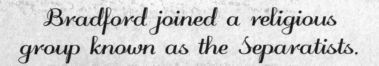

Bradford joined a religious group known as the Separatists.

Then he met William Brewster in the nearby town of Scrooby. Bradford went to a church service at Brewster's home and found just what he had been looking for. Led by a young minister named John Robinson, the people believed that faith (religious belief) and discipline should touch every part of their lives. They also thought that the Church of England, with its fancy rituals and ceremonies, was not a true church.

It was this last belief that forced the group, known as Separatists, to meet in secret. England's King James I was the head of the Church of England, and he saw the Separatists as a threat.

When the congregation was discovered, some members were thrown in prison, and others were harassed. It was time for the group, including 17-year-old William Bradford, to leave England.

England's King James I saw the Separatists as a threat.

Cross-staff

To use a cross-staff, a navigator held the stick just below eye level. He slid a crosspiece until the top of it aligned with the sun or stars and the bottom with the horizon. Once the angle was known, the navigator could use charts and maps to work out latitude.

A cross-staff could determine latitude within a few miles.

The *Mayflower* had only managed to sail 3.2 km per hour (2 miles per hour) since leaving England.

Why so slow?

Master Jones didn't know this, but the *Mayflower* was sailing against the Gulf Stream. It is a huge current of warm water that flows up from the Caribbean. The current pushed against the *Mayflower* as it sailed.

Many passengers slept in hammocks.

Below deck

When seas were calm, the passengers walked on deck to get exercise. But most of the time, they were stuck down below. To pass the time, everyone played simple games, read, told stories, and sang. This could not have been pleasant because the 'tween deck, where they stayed, was damp, dark, and stuffy.

The 'tween deck

The 'tween deck was about 23 m (75 ft) long with low ceilings. There were no windows or cabins. Some people chose to sleep in a large boat up on deck. Others hired the ship's carpenter to build walls. This did give them some privacy, but it also made it stuffier and more crowded than before.

Hardtack biscuits

A baby was born during the journey. He was named Oceanus.

People put their possessions in hanging baskets to save space.

Food on board

Mealtime was no picnic either. It was dangerous to light a fire, which meant hot food was a rare treat. Instead, people usually ate salted beef, hardtack (dried biscuits), dried vegetables, beans, and cheese.

The water on board wasn't fresh at all. People became ill when they drank it, so they drank beer instead.

North America

Cape Cod

After two months, they finally saw the shores of North America.

Land ahoy!

On 9 November, 1620, land was finally within sight!
After more than two months at sea, the passengers
looked upon the sandy beach and celebrated.
Sailors who had been here before knew the
Mayflower had reached Cape Cod.

But the Pilgrims' patent was for land 320 km (200 miles)
further south. It would be illegal for them to settle here,
but the other passengers wanted to stay. So the two
groups debated about what to do. They decided to
sail onwards. With no maps of the shoreline to guide
him, Master Jones headed the ship down the coast.

For the first five hours of the journey, everything went smoothly. Then the *Mayflower* reached the sharp elbow of the Cape and sailed straight into a churning sea – an area called Pollock Rip. Shallow sandbars and roaring waves threatened to tear the ship apart.

For the next hour and a half, Master Jones fought to keep the ship afloat. Then the winds calmed and he was able to turn the ship around and escape. The *Mayflower*, he decided, would head back north.

Atlantic Ocean

First landing of the *Mayflower*

Provincetown Harbor

Plymouth

The Mayflower tried to sail south, but had to turn back.

Cape Cod Bay

Cape Cod

N
W   E
S

Even today, the unpredictable nature of this area makes navigating its waters a challenge.

Pollock Rip

The area where the *Mayflower* nearly sank is known as Pollock Rip.

The Mayflower Compact

As the ship headed back north, people began to protest. The Pilgrims had a deep religious bond holding them together, and many Strangers had strong ties to the Adventurers. But the settlers were now outside of their legal patent, and they needed to create a new set of laws.

If the colony was going to succeed, everyone on board would have to get along and help out. For that to happen, they needed some sort of formal agreement that bound them together as a community. They had to set up rules, laws, and government. Only half of the people on board were Pilgrims. Because of this, they decided to form a civil government run by the people. The government would not be based on religion.

The passengers set to work and wrote an agreement called the Mayflower Compact. On November 11, 1620, before anyone even set foot on shore, 41 adult male passengers signed it. This included all the men planning to stay who were healthy enough to sign their names. It laid down the rules and laws of the new colony. That same day, John Carver was confirmed as the first governor of the new settlement.

"In the name of God, Amen.
We whose names are underwritten, the loyal
subjects of our dread sovereign Lord, King
James...having undertaken, for the glory of
God...a voyage to plant the first colony in the
Northern parts of Virginia, do...covenant and
combine ourselves together into a civil body politic,
for our better ordering and preservation and
furtherance of the ends aforesaid; and by virtue
hereof to enact, constitute, and frame such just
and equal laws, ordinances, acts, constitutions,
and offices, from time to time, as shall be
thought most meet and convenient for the
general good of the colony..."

The arrival

While the passengers were busy creating their new government, Master Jones sailed the *Mayflower* into Provincetown Harbour. The ship was now safely anchored in one of the biggest natural harbours in all of New England.

Provincetown Harbour

For the first time in months, it was safe for the passengers to walk on the ship's upper deck, escaping the stench and filth down below. The fresh air was welcome, but the landscape before them was disappointing. The ground was low and sandy. It was not a good place to build their new settlement.

That first day, 16 men took a rowing boat to shore. When they reached land, the men explored their new surroundings. When they came back, they described what they had seen – marshy ponds, low trees, and thousands of birds.

Women washed laundry.

The *Mayflower* was safely anchored.

28

The missing people

Before the Pilgrims arrived, it is thought that between 50,000 to 100,000 Wampanoag People lived in the area where the *Mayflower* landed. One of these indigenous groups was the Pokanoket. Massasoit was their sachem, or most powerful leader. Diseases brought by European explorers had swept through the land, killing nearly three quarters of the Pokanokets. The entire village of Patuxet, where the Pilgrims eventually founded Plymouth Colony, was wiped out by the plague. Massasoit, who would later play an important role in the Pilgrims' story, survived.

The Mayflower anchored in the harbour.

Passengers rowed to shore.

The next day was a Sunday and everyone stayed on board the *Mayflower* to worship. But by Monday, it was time for the work to begin. Some men continued to explore. Others brought pieces of the shallop (a large, open boat) to shore so that the carpenter could put it back together. The boat had been taken apart and stored on the 'tween deck during the voyage. Women washed laundry on the shore and children ran along the beach.

Some passengers had been so eager to set foot on land that they waded through the icy waters to get there. In the coming days, that would lead to colds, coughs, and sickness that spread among the people.

The passengers were eager to get to shore.

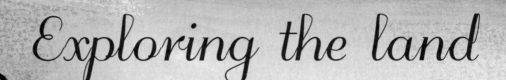

Exploring the land

Winter was fast approaching. Everyone knew they needed to quickly find a place to build their settlement. Some had seen the mouth of a river when they first sailed into the harbour – that was a promising place to explore.

The Native Americans travelled with a dog.

For days, the men followed

On Wednesday 15 November, 16 men, led by Captain Myles Standish, rowed to shore. The armed men marched down the freezing beach. After a mile or so, they saw five or six people and a dog coming toward them. When the people ran for the woods, the *Mayflower* men realised that they had just seen Native Americans. They wanted to talk to them.

The *Mayflower* men carried weapons.

They followed the people for miles but, still weak from the voyage, they couldn't catch up. So they built a fire, posted guards, and settled in for the night. For two more days, the men followed the Native Americans' tracks through the woods.

the Native Americans' tracks through the woods.

They never saw them again, but they did discover a freshwater stream. They also saw the remains of a European fort. They found unoccupied Wampanoag homes, which they explored; graves, which they dug up; and baskets filled with corn, which they took. Then they made their way back to the ship.

Wampanoag homes

First encounter

A few days later, the shallop was fixed. Master Jones and 34 men set out to explore along the harbour. For two days, they searched for a new home while snow fell heavily and temperatures dropped.

The settlers took what they wanted from unoccupied villages as they explored.

When the men found more corn, some of them returned to the warmth of the *Mayflower*. Captain Standish and the remaining men continued the search on land. They spent another night in the woods. The next day, they trampled through the snow, hoping to find a good place to build their settlement. Each time they discovered an unoccupied village, they sorted through it, taking what they liked.

The men returned to the *Mayflower*, and a few days later, they set out again. But their days of looting had not gone unnoticed. Near midnight, the men were startled by a terrible cry.

They grabbed their muskets, but couldn't see anyone. Early the next morning, arrows from at least 30 Wampanoag men flew their way.

The men boarded the shallop again and sailed through choppy, freezing waters. Just as all seemed to be lost, they found a small island in a protected cove. The water was deep enough for a big ship like the *Mayflower*. The mainland had several streams and was good for farming. And there were no signs of Native Americans. They had found their new home – Plymouth, Massachusetts.

Back on the Mayflower...

While the men were out exploring, all was not quiet on the *Mayflower*. A young passenger called Francis Billington shot his father's gun inside the cabin. Sparks flew towards an open barrel of gunpowder. Francis nearly destroyed the ship! The cycle of life and death continued as well. A baby boy named Peregrine was born. And four passengers died, including William Bradford's wife, Dorothy, who fell from the ship and drowned.

Plymouth

Provincetown Harbour

Cape Cod Bay

Second landing of the *Mayflower*

A new home

The settlers found the cornfields of Patuxet while they were exploring. There were no Wampanoags living there because they had either died of disease brought by Europeans or moved to another village. The deserted cornfields looked like a good place for a new home.

33

A difficult winter

In late December, the Pilgrims began planning the layout of their new settlement. Then, they built their first building – a common house. Once that was finished, they started building small wooden homes. Cannons from the *Mayflower* were also brought ashore. The people worked as quickly as they could because they needed shelter before the worst of winter set in. But the long voyage had taken its toll. Supplies were low and many people were weak from hunger or diseases such as scurvy.

Many settlers suffered from scurvy, a disease that people get when they don't eat enough fresh fruits and vegetables.

Within three months, half of those who had made the journey on the *Mayflower* were dead. Sometimes, two or three people died on the same day. Christopher Martin, the governor of the *Mayflower*, was among the victims. Nearly everyone had lost someone they loved.

As winter dragged on, the Pilgrims struggled to survive. Before long, Native Americans were spotted in the distance. The Pilgrims knew they were being watched, and they were worried. Would their shrinking numbers encourage the Wampanoag men to attack? Just in case, they put Captain Standish in charge of their militia (men chosen to fight). Although the Pilgrims had run into Wampanoag men a few times, nothing had prepared them for what happened next.

Forging a friendship

On 16 March, 1621, a Native American man approached the settlement. His name was Samoset. He had been sent by Massasoit, sachem (leader) of the Pokanoket, to meet with the Pilgrims. They had been watching the Pilgrims and saw that these settlers were different from European explorers who had come before.

The Wampanoags knew that the Pilgrims weren't there to capture or kill – they meant to stay. Samoset spoke to them in English about the people and land around them. He also told them about Massasoit's hope that they would become friends. Then he left. He returned a few days later with several men. One of them was a man named Tisquantum, or Squanto, who spoke English even better than Samoset did.

A few hours later, Massasoit came too. He had 60 men with him. Massasoit met with Governor Carver, and the two men worked out an alliance (agreement) stating how their people would work together. They would help and protect each other if either came under attack. The Pilgrims agreed to pay back the people whose corn they had stolen months before. And Squanto would stay with the Pilgrims to help translate and teach them how to survive. The agreement stood even after Governor Carver died a few months later and William Bradford was elected to take his place.

Governor Carver and Massasoit worked out an agreement.

Moving forward

Two weeks later, the *Mayflower* sailed back to England. The Adventurers had expected the ship to be filled with riches and resources from the land. Instead, the ship carried just a few artefacts, and its hold was filled with stones.

Many people had died, and the Adventurers had little to show for all the money they had invested. But despite all the hardships they had faced, none of the remaining Pilgrims returned with the ship. One crew member even decided to stay with the Pilgrims.

The sad fate of the *Mayflower*

After returning to England, Master Jones sailed the *Mayflower* to France. Shortly after his return, he died. Jones had been a part owner of the ship, so after his death, the *Mayflower* sat unused, rotting in the harbour. By 1624, just four years after its historic voyage to North America, it was in ruins. Most likely, it was sold off as scrap.

Over the next few months, the Pilgrims listened and learned. Squanto introduced them to the fish that swam in the fresh waters. He showed them how to plant corn, burying dead fish in the soil so the crops would grow even better. He taught them how to grow other native crops too. This was important, because the seeds the Pilgrims had brought from England struggled to grow in the new environment.

The Pilgrims learned how to grow native crops.

As the new governor, William Bradford continued to build trust with Massasoit. The two groups hosted each other often. And after Massasoit spread word of their alliance, other communities agreed to cooperate with the Pilgrims as well.

The first Thanksgiving

In the autumn of 1621, the Pilgrims celebrated their first successful harvest, which was an English tradition. The 52 remaining Pilgrims had much to be thankful for, having survived a harsh winter and formed alliances with the Wampanoag People. Nobody knows exactly when the celebration took place, but we do know that it lasted for three days.

The Pilgrims feasted on fruits and vegetables they had gathered. They ate ducks, geese, wild turkeys, fish, and other seafood. When Massasoit and 90 other Wampanoags arrived, they added five freshly killed deer to the meal. Everybody played games and celebrated. Nobody called it "Thanksgiving", but everyone gave thanks.

The Thanksgiving holiday
that Americans celebrate
today is based on the first
Thanksgiving at Plymouth.

The Mayflower II

The *Mayflower* is a powerful symbol. It represents hope, determination, and people's basic need for freedom. The original ship is long gone. But since 1957, another vessel has stood in its place: the *Mayflower II*.

The *Mayflower II* is a reproduction of the original ship that sailed in 1620. The new ship was built between 1955 and 1957 in Brixham, England. It represents the friendship shared between the UK and the United States during World War II.

Like the original *Mayflower*, the *Mayflower II* sailed from Plymouth, England, to Plymouth, Massachusetts.

On April 4, 1957, the *Mayflower II* took its first voyage around Brixham Bay in England.